AF428241

The Great Things You Will Be

written by:

Dr. Terrica Rumph

illustrated by:

Kimberly Martinez

To my son, Brayden, who is the inspiration behind this book. You are and always will be my world. You bring me such joy, and I can't wait to watch you grow into the amazing man I know you will be someday.

I love you, son.

Love,
Your mom

The Great Things You Will Be

Oh, my sweet baby,
I can't wait to see

all of the great things
that you will be.

Maybe you will be
a teacher, a lawyer,
a doctor, or an athlete.

BA BY

You will be the greatest person
that anyone did meet.

You will be important,
and you will be smart.

SHAPES
LETTERS

You will care
for others right
from the start.

Q
Q
Q
K
K
K

You will strive to be kind
and you will be a leader
who keeps others in mind.

You will be
happy and confident.

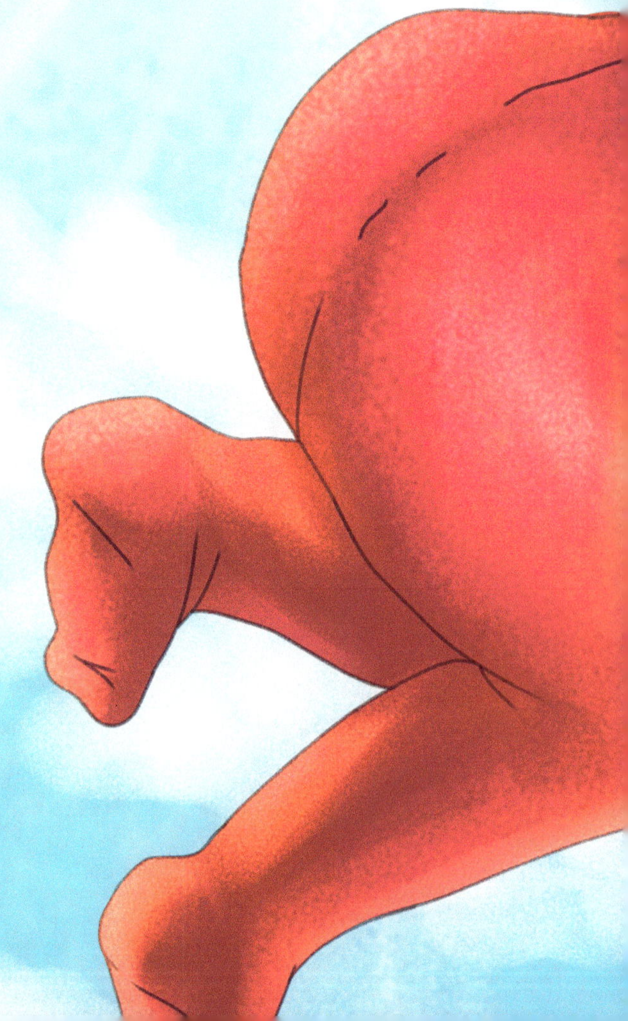

You will believe in yourself.

You will understand the importance of maintaining good health.

BABY

You will be a positive person,
and you will be strong.

You will be respectful of others and admit when you are wrong.

Oh, my sweet baby,
I can't wait to see

how truly great of
a person you will be.

Dear Readers,

I would like to express my sincerest gratitude to you for purchasing this book. Thank you so much for your love and support. I hope that this book sparks inspiration in your little one at an early age and that they smile when they see the illustrations.

If your little one enjoys this book, I ask that you leave an honest review to let other readers know your honest opinion. Please visit my website and follow the link to leave a review.

Your comments and reviews mean so much to me and help other readers determine what books to get next.

Again, I thank you!

Love, Terrica Rumph
www.terricarumph.com

Terrica Rumph is a native of Montgomery, Alabama but currently resides in Atlanta, Georgia where she practices as a Nurse Practitioner. She is a co-host of a health and wellness podcast and is a co-founder of a scholarship for high school students.

Terrica is a caring wife and mother of 1. She has always aspired to become an author. Shortly after having her first child, she began speaking positive affirmations over her son. She realized how important this was and the idea to write a children's book was created.

Terrica enjoys spending time with her family, traveling, photography, DIY projects, real estate investing, and partnering with brands to create content in her spare time.

Dr. Terrica Rumph